Scragscutt

Dr Barnardo

Miss Baker

Jonathan

Rachel

The Maid

a

Lisa

Harry

Beth

## Beth
Harry's younger sister. She is always hungry because she doesn't get enough to eat. She is very scared of Scragscutt.

## Scragscutt
A villain who tricks Harry and Beth into cleaning chimneys, and then pockets the money they earn. He is cruel and ruthless.

## Maid
A short-tempered girl who has to keep a rich person's house clean and tidy.

## Dr Barnardo
A well-dressed, kindly gentleman who sets out to help street orphans.

*Place: a classroom.*

*Time: the present day.*

*There is a general hubbub of chatter and nor as the class awaits the teacher. The children sitting in groups; Ajeeta, Jonathan, Rachel and Lisa are sitting together at a table.*

**Miss Baker:** *(Entering the classroom and clapping her hands)* Right! Quiet, everyone! Our lesso is History, and we'll be studying the Victorians. I want each group to find out about the "working children". Ajeeta, he are the books for your group.

*(Miss Baker hands Ajeeta four or five referen books. There is chatter.)*

**Rachel:** What's she mean, the working children?

**Lisa:** *We're* working children, aren't we? School's nothing but work, work, and more work!

**Rachel:** Long time since *you* did any school work Lisa.

**Ajeeta:** All right, you two. Stop arguing. Miss Baker means the working children from Victorian times.

4

**Rachel:** And when was that, know-all?

**Ajeeta:** About a century ago. Eighteen hundred and something. It was when children of our age had to work in factories –

**Jonathan:** And down the mines –

**Ajeeta:** And sweep chimneys.

**Lisa:** Ugh! Cleaning soot and muck out of chimneys! Those kids must have been filthy!

**Ajeeta & Jonathan:** They were!

**Ajeeta:** Look, here are pictures of them in this book.

**Jonathan:** They look about eight or nine years old. Same as us.

**Ajeeta:** And lots of them were orphans.

| | |
|---|---|
| **Lisa:** | Orph-what? |
| **Ajeeta:** | Orphans. No parents. No mum, no dad. |
| **Jonathan:** | *(Pointing to pictures in the book)* And no homes, by the look of things. It says here … "many orphans lived and slept c the streets in towns and cities." |
| **Rachel:** | So, what did they eat? How did they survive? |
| **Ajeeta:** | They had to find work. That's why they were called working children. |
| **Jonathan:** | Or they begged. |
| **Lisa:** | Or stole, I bet. |
| **Ajeeta:** | It must have been a terrible life. No food, no parents, living on the streets … and having to find work to earn some money. |
| **Jonathan:** | And no older than us. |
| **Lisa:** | Oh, this is all cheering me up no end! Mis Baker's given us a really brill subject this time! |
| **Ajeeta:** | Stop moaning, Lisa. We've got work to dc so let's get on with it. |
| | *(Low hubbub of voices as the children work.)* |
| **Miss Baker:** | Not too much noise, please. Everyone settle down. Get on with your work. |
| | *(The noise fades to silence.)* |

*Place: a busy street.*

*Time: a century ago (Victorian times).*

*Street cries can be heard: "Fresh Fish!", "Rosy red apples!", "Cats' meat!", "Spanish onions!", "Shoes and boots repaired!", "Flowers, fresh-cut flowers!"*

*People pass by along the street. Harry and Beth, two hungry orphans, try to attract their attention.*

**Harry:** Spare a farthing! Give us a farthing!

**Beth:** Anything for a starving girl? A crust of bread?

**Harry:** Spare a farthing, Guv? Give us a farthin

**Beth:** Anything for a hungry girl, lady? Anything?

**Harry:** Spare a farthing! Give us a farthing!

**Beth:** Anything for a starving girl? A crust of bread?

**First lady:** What disgusting urchins!

**Second lady:** They're everywhere. The town's full of brats begging.

**First lady:** (*Pointing*) Just look at those children! Jus look at their clothes!

**Second lady** Call those *clothes*? Nothing but rags, filthy rags.

**First lady:** And their feet are bare. And what *horrible* feet! Ugh!

**Second lady:** Don't go near them. You'll catch a disease Come on.

*(They pass by.)*

**Harry:** Spare a farthing!

**Beth:** Got a crust of bread? Just a crust of stale bread?

**Harry:** Give us a farthing, Guv?

*(A grim-looking man stops and then walks slowly round the children, as if inspecting them.)*

**Scragscutt:** And who are you two, eh? What's with all this shouting, eh?

**Harry:** We're begging, sir. We're hungry. This is my young sister, Beth, and she's –

**Beth:** Starving!

**Scragscutt:** Hungry are you? Starving, eh? And what are your parents doing about it? Why aren't they looking after you, eh?

**Harry:** Our parents are dead, sir. We're orphans.

**Scragscutt:** Orphans … well now, isn't that just one big surprise. Orphans, eh? And you've got no food.

**Harry:** That's right, sir.

**Scragscutt:** And you've got no money.

**Beth:** That's right, sir.

**Scragscutt:** Well, maybe I can help you. Have you ... er ... ever worked, eh?

**Harry:** Worked? No, sir. We're too young.

**Scragscutt:** Oh, you're never too young, lad. Maybe can teach you to work. Yes, I'm sure you like to earn some money ... and to have good dinner, wouldn't you, eh?

**Harry:** Oh, yes, sir.

**Scragscutt:** And how old are you?

**Harry:** I'm nine –

**Beth:** And I'm eight.

**Scragscutt:** Just right! Just the ticket! Look, you two youngsters follow me and I'll ... er ... fin a place for you to stay. And I'll ... er ... find you a job of work. Heh, heh! You'll soon learn how to work, how to work hard! You call me Scragscutt. That's all you need to know. Just follow me ...

*(He exits, followed by Harry and Beth.)*

**Harry:** Where are we, sir?

**Scragscutt:** My house, lad, my house.

**Harry:** It's a bit of a ruin, isn't it?

**Scragscutt:** Ruin? Nah. It's a real home from home. Now, you two'll sleep down there, down those steps, in the cellar.

11

**Beth:**   It looks a bit cold …

**Harry:**   And a bit wet …

**Scragscutt:**   Complaining already are we, eh? Well, don't fret. You'll be so tired working for me, you won't care *where* you sleep.

**Harry:**   What kind of work is it, sir?

**Beth:**   And when do we get something to eat?

**Harry:**   When do we start?

**Beth:**   Can I have a crust of bread now?

**Scragscutt:**   Questions, questions, questions. Nothing but what's this and what's that. Look, brats, you work first … and then you eat. All right? So, let's get going. Girl, pick up those sacks. You, boy, grab that bundle of brushes.

**Harry:**   These are brushes for sweeping chimneys

**Scragscutt:** How right you are, lad. And that's just what you're going to be. Chimney-sweeps.

**Beth:** But I've never been inside a chimney.

**Scragscutt:** You soon will. You'll learn, both of you, and no mistake. You're so skinny you'll have no trouble climbing inside chimneys. Right, off we go.

**Harry:** Where to, sir?

**Scragscutt:** A big house, a big posh house. So mind your manners. You do as I say and you'll get –

**Harry:** Money?

**Beth:** And food?

**Scragscutt:** But work first, eh? Work first. Now, keep up with me and no lagging behind.

*(Scragscutt sets off. The children struggle along behind him, carrying the brushes and the soot sacks. They arrive at the big house.)*

**Scragscutt:** Here we are, here we are. *(He rubs his hands.)* Six chimneys! Oh yes, this will make a pretty penny. *(He rubs his hands again and pulls the rope connected to the doorbell.)*

**Maid:** *(Opening the door)* Yes? What do you want

**Scragscutt:** Scragscutt. Chimney sweep. I was booked

**Maid:** Oh, yes, I remember. Those dirty urchins with you?

**Scragscutt:** Indeed they are. Couple of strong and willing workers.

**Maid:** They don't look very strong to me. Look as if they could do with a good dinner –

**Scragscutt:** Shhh! Never mention f-o-o-d, ma'am. Takes their minds off the job in hand. Now, let's have a look at your chimneys.

**Maid:** And no mess, mind. Her Ladyship will be mad as a wild cat if there's as much as a smudge of soot on her furniture.

**Scragscutt:** Ma'am never fear. Scragscutt's here! *(He turns to the children.)* Come on, brats. Follow me, and careful with those brushes. Look lively!

*(They follow the maid offstage.)*

**Scragscutt:** Everything's ready. Okay, Harry boy, up the chimney you go. And make sure you get *all* that soot brushed down.

**Harry:** Then can we have something to eat?

**Scragscutt:** Haven't I said so? Go on!

*(He pushes the boy. Harry starts to mime climbing up the chimney.)*

**Scragscutt:** And now you girl. Up there … after your brother.

*(He pushes Beth, who climbs up the chimney.)*

**Maid:** Are you sure they'll be all right?

**Scragscutt:** Course they will, ma'am.

**Maid:** But they've got bare feet.

**Scragscutt:** All the better for climbing in the darkness. Helps them to feel for the bricks.

**Maid:** A bit young, aren't they?

**Scragscutt:** So what? Younger the better, I always say. Train 'em while they're young, eh?

**Maid:** You'll not make a mess?

**Scragscutt:** Course not. Cross my heart and hope to die.

**Maid:** Like a mug of tea, would you?

**Scragscutt:** Lovely! Six sugars, ma'am, if you please.

*(Meanwhile, Harry is climbing higher inside the chimney. Beth is not far behind).)*

**Harry:** Beth, are you all right?

**Beth:** I think so, but it's scary.

**Harry:** Make sure your feet don't slip.

**Beth:** It's terribly dark. And horribly smelly. There's thick soot everywhere.

**Harry:** I'm starting to brush now. Keep you head down. Here goes!

*(Harry grunts as he sweeps.)*

**Beth:** Harry! Soot's falling all over me! It's in my eyes and hair. I can taste it in my mouth!

**Harry:** Then climb up beside me. We'll have to sweep together. Sooner we finish the sooner we get something to eat.

**Beth:** We're very high up.

**Harry:** You still scared?

**Beth:** Can't stop shaking.

**Harry:** Hey, what's this? Twigs … and sticks. Must be the remains of a bird's nest.

**Beth:** Ugh, it stinks!

**Harry:** Just keep on climbing. Watch you don't slip. Hey, look up there. A patch of blue … blue sky. We're nearly at the top.

**Beth:** I'm sore all over. I think my feet are bleeding.

**Harry:** Same here. But we're almost at the top. Just one big shove … and the brush is out of the chimney pot. We've done it! We can climb back down.

**Scragscutt:** (*Shouting up the chimney*) You brats up there! You lazy brats! Get down here now! You've got another five chimneys to clean. Hurry up!

**Beth:** *More* chimneys!

**Harry:** 'Fraid so, sister.

**Beth:** But I'm tired, and starving hungry.

**Harry:** Rest for a minute. You'll feel better.

**Scragscutt:** I warned you! I warned you to get a move on! I'll smoke you out!

**Beth:** What does he mean, smoke us out?

**Harry:** He's burning paper, starting a fire, that's what he means. Watch out, here comes the smoke. *(He starts to cough.)* Come on, Beth, climb down as quickly as you can!

**Beth:** *(Also coughing)* I can hardly breathe.

**Harry:** Hurry! The smoke's getting worse!

*(They scramble out of the chimney and tumble into the room.)*

**Scragscutt:** *(Grabbing the children)* And about time too. What do you think this is, your holiday, eh? You've got the next chimney to sweep, so move yourselves!

*(Scragscutt marches them out of the room.)*

**Harry:** What a day! I'm utterly exhausted.

**Beth:** I feel half dead. *Begging* is better than working for Scragscutt.

**Harry:** And after all that chimney-sweeping, what did we get?

**Beth:** A bowl of weak soup, a hunk of mouldy bread and two green potatoes. I'm *still* starving.

**Harry:** Me too. And it's freezing cold down here in this cellar.

**Beth:** And the straw's damp. We'll get pneumonia.

**Harry:** Listen, what's that?

**Beth:** What?

**Harry:** That … scratching. It's a rat!

*(Beth shrieks, then starts to cry)*

**Harry:** That does it. Let's get out of here. Sleeping in the streets is better than this. Come on, Beth, let's escape.

**Beth:** But Scragscutt locked the door.

**Harry:** Then we'll just have to smash it down. Come on.

*(They creep up the cellar steps.)*

**Harry:** We'll ram the door with our shoulders. Ready? One, two, three!

*(The door bursts open. Scragscutt calls out from offstage.)*

**Scragscutt:** Hey, you! Hey, get back down that cellar

**Harry:** Not on your life, Scragscutt. We're going

**Beth:** And we won't be back!

**Scragscutt:** Come here, you brats. Get back down th: cellar, you devils!

**Harry:** Goodbye, and next time clean the rotten old chimneys your rotten old self!

*(They run away.)*

**Scragscutt:** *(Coming on stage)* There's thanks, eh? There's gratitude, eh? I give them shelter and a bed, and a dinner. And what do they do? Scarper! Well, they'll come to nc good, that's for sure. They'll end up in th gutter … dead. I'll get some more orphan tomorrow. Plenty to choose from, that's for sure, eh?

## Scene 6

*Place: a busy street.*

*Time: Victorian times (the next day).*

*Street cries can be heard: "Fresh Fish!", "Rosy red apples!", "Cats' meat!", "Spanish onions!", "Shoes and boots repaired!", "Flowers, fresh-cut flowers!"*

*People pass by along the street as Harry and Beth try to attract their attention.*

**Harry:** Spare a farthing! Give us a farthing!

**Beth:** Anything for a starving girl? A crust of bread?

**Harry:** Spare a farthing, Guv? Give us a farthing!

**Beth:** Anything for a hungry girl, lady? Anything?

*(A man approaches.)*

**Man:** You two are doing a lot of shouting. What's the matter?

**Harry:** We won't work like slaves, if that's what you're after.

**Beth:** You won't get us back up those chimneys

**Man:** What's all this? Slaves? Chimneys?

**Harry:** No more sweeping chimneys!

**Beth:** And that's final, so there!

**Man:** Dear me, you *do* seem upset, you *do* seem angry.

**Harry:** Well, you'd be angry, wouldn't you?

**Man:** Would I? Why?

**Beth:** If you'd been forced to sweep chimneys …
for a mouthful of food.

**Man:** Indeed I would be angry. No one should
be forced to do *that* sort of work. And
certainly not children. How old are you?

**Harry:** I'm nine –

**Beth:** And I'm eight.

**Harry:** And we're orphans.

**Beth:** And we're hungry.

**Man:** I see. I think perhaps you'd better come
with me.

**Harry:** No fear! We've already fallen for that trick!
Scragscutt and his chimney-sweeping was
quite enough, thank you.

**Man:** Scragscutt. I've heard of him. A real villain by all accounts. Run away from him, have you? *(The children nod.)* Look, I'm not asking you to work. I'm inviting you to my home.

**Harry:** To your home?

**Beth:** But … why?

**Man:** Because I believe it's wrong for orphans be roaming the streets, begging. And no child should be sweeping chimneys. Certainly not. So, I have founded a home a special home, for orphans.

**Harry:** That the truth?

**Man:** It's the whole truth, and nothing but the truth.

**Beth:** Cross your heart?

**Man:** Cross my heart. By the way, what are you names?

**Harry:** I'm Harry –

**Beth:** And I'm Beth.

**Harry:** And your name, sir?

**Man:** Barnardo. Doctor Barnardo. Come on, it's time for you to meet my family.

**Miss Baker:** *(Clapping her hands)* Right, stop work everyone! The bell will ring for break time in a minute. I hope you've all finished your work. Have you?

**Class:** Yes, Miss Baker.

**Miss Baker:** Good. Well, you should now know a great deal about the working children in Victorian days. I hope so, anyway. We have time for one question. Is there one?

**Ajeeta:** I've a question, Miss.

**Miss Baker:** Yes, Ajeeta.

**Ajeeta:** We found out about a man called Doctor Barnardo. Is it true he set up a special home for orphans and homeless children?

**Miss Baker:** Quite true.

**Ajeeta:** Are they the Barnardo's Homes we have today?

**Miss Baker:** Indeed they are, Ajeeta. The work that Doctor Barnardo began a century ago continues today. Quite an achievement, don't you agree?

**Ajeeta:** Yes, Miss Baker.

*(A bell rings.)*

**Miss Baker:** Break time! Perfect timing! All of you, ou to play.

*(The children exit, talking, laughing, pushing and joking. Ajeeta is finishing some writing.)*

**Jonathan:** Come on, Ajeeta, or we'll be last out.

**Ajeeta:** Nearly finished this writing … there. All done.

**Jonathan:** *(As they leave the classroom)* What are we going to play today?

**Ajeeta:** How about … climbing chimneys!

*(They exit.)*

## Choosing Parts
The parts of Harry, Beth and Scragscutt should be read by confident readers. Miss Baker and her class, the Maid and Dr Barnardo are less demanding.

## Putting On the Play
You may wish to put on a performance of the play, rather than just reading it. The following suggestions may provide you with a starting point for your own ideas about staging a production. Obviously, the use you make of these suggestions will vary depending on the time and resources available to your school.

**For permission to put on a profit-making performance of *The Working Children*, please contact the Editorial Department, Ginn & Co. Ltd, Prebendal House, Parson's Fee, Aylesbury, Bucks HP20 2QY.**
(There is no need to apply for permission if you are not charging an entrance fee, but please let us know if you are putting on any performance of this play, as we would be interested to hear about it.)

### Staging
The play takes place in seven locations:
- a present-day classroom;
- a busy Victorian street;
- behind a tumbledown house;
- outside a big house;
- inside the big house;
- inside the chimney;
- inside the cellar of Scragscutt's house.

The action then returns to the busy street, and then finally to the present-day classroom. Dividing the stage into so many different locations would place great demands on the space. However, the stage divisions could be made more manageable.

The classroom could be set in an upstage corner. The street scene would then be played on the main stage area before Scragscutt leads the children to a small shelter downstage (perhaps a large cardboard box) to represent the cellar. Centre stage could then be the pavement outside the big house, and the other upstage corner would then represent the chimney. The action returns to the cellar, the street and the classroom.

An alternative approach, giving more opportunity for flexibility and invention, would be to set the classroom scene centre stage, and thereafter use the characters and furniture of that scene to change the locations. A table could be used to raise Harry above Beth as they climb the chimney, while Scragscutt lurks below.

A gymnastically-inclined class could even form a 'living chimney' for Harry and Beth to climb! The cellar could be represented by a table as well, with Harry and Beth beneath it, and the door could be formed by two members of Miss Baker's class.

### Costumes
**Harry** and **Beth** should wear caps and ragged clothes. They would have bare feet.
The **First** and **Second Ladies** will need long dresses, bonnets and baskets.
**Scragscutt** can have an old suit with a heavy belt and boots, a neckerchief and a knobbly stick.
The **Maid** will wear a black dress with a white apron and a cap.
**Dr Barnardo** will need an overcoat and

walking stick, and a top hat if possible. The **present-day characters** can wear contemporary clothes.

## Props
A pile of reference books and some tables and chairs will be needed for the modern classroom scene.

For the scenes in the cellar and the chimney-sweeping scene you will need a bundle of old sacks and some brushes (or you could use old broom handles or lengths of bamboo).

NB - the sticks and newspaper used by Scragscutt to light the fire could constitute a fire hazard and might be better mimed!

For the scene on the doorstep of the big house you might like to provide a rope with a bell attached, though this could be mimed to the sound of an offstage bell.

For the final classroom scene you will need a handbell to signal the end of the lesson.

## Follow-up Work

## Research
You could encourage the children to find out about the following:
- the position of orphan and foundling children in Victorian society;
- the Ragged Schools;
- child labour in mines and factories, the Factory Acts;
- workhouses, outdoor relief, the Poor Laws.

Television adaptations of Dickens can provide useful material for this, and many schools have already done extensive work on the Victorian education system.

You might also like to study the work of Dr Barnardo and the subsequent history of the Homes he set up.

## Drama
### Hot-seating
Hot-seating is a strategy which can help pupils either to create a character or to develop greater understanding of a character in the text.

1. Put a chair at the front of the class and arange the rest of the class in a semicircle around it.
2. Choose a child to represent one of the characters in the play, and ask him or her to sit in the hot seat.
3. The rest of the class must ask the child questions, which he or she has to answer in role – in other words, as the character.

The object is to explore the characters' motivation for acting as they do.

You could interview the First and Second Ladies, the Maid and Scragscutt in this way, but you might also bring in other characters; perhaps Harry and Beth have an aunt or uncle who has refused to look after them.

### Judgement Chair
After you have asked questions of each character, each member of the group should pronounce judgement on that character. For example, "It's all very well for you to sneer at orphans – you're rich!"